The Emperors of the Roman Empire
Biography History Books | Children's Historical Biographies

Speedy Publishing LLC
40 E. Main St. #1156
Newark, DE 19711
www.speedypublishing.com

Copyright 2017

All Rights reserved. No part of this book may be reproduced or used in any way or form or by any means whether electronic or mechanical, this means that you cannot record or photocopy any material ideas or tips that are provided in this book

During the first 500 years of Ancient Rome, the Roman government consisted of a republic where no one person had the ultimate power. During the next 500 years, however, it became ruled by an emperor. Even though many republic governmental offices were still there, such as senators, to assist with running the government, the emperor was considered its supreme leader and even sometimes referred to as their god.

THE FIRST ROMAN EMPEROR

Caesar Augustus was Rome's first Emperor. He went by other names, including Octavius, but then became Augustus when he became their emperor. He had become the adopted heir to Julius Caesar.

Caesar Augustus

Julius Caesar had paved the road for this Roman Republic to be an Empire. He had a very good army and had become known as a very powerful emperor. When they defeated Pompey the Great during a civil war, they made him dictator. However, some of the Romans wanted the government republic to be placed back in power.

Just after he was made dictator, in 44 BC, he was assassinated by Marcus Brutus. However, this new republic did not last long since Caesar's heir, Octavius, had already become quite powerful himself. He then took over for Caesar and went on to become the Roman Empire's first Emperor.

Caesar Augustus

Julius Caesar

Julius Caesar had paved the road for this Roman Republic to be an Empire. He had a very good army and had become known as a very powerful emperor. When they defeated Pompey the Great during a civil war, they made him dictator. However, some of the Romans wanted the government republic to be placed back in power.

Just after he was made dictator, in 44 BC, he was assassinated by Marcus Brutus. However, this new republic did not last long since Caesar's heir, Octavius, had already become quite powerful himself. He then took over for Caesar and went on to become the Roman Empire's first Emperor.

STRONG EMPERORS

At first thought you might believe that moving from the Roman republic to being led by an Emperor would be a bad idea. This was true in some cases. In other cases, however, since the Emperor was known to be a strong, good leader, he would bring prosperity and peace to Rome. Here is a listing of some of the better Roman Emperors:

Caesar Augustus

He was born in Rome, Italy on September 23, 63 BC and died in Nola, Italy on August 19, 14 AD. His reign lasted from 27 BC to 14 AD. The first Emperor, known as Augustus, would provide a great example for those who followed.

After the years of war in Rome, his rule became the Pax Romana, the time of peace. He established a network of roads, rebuilt a lot of the city of Rome, and a standing army. He ruled until his death when Tiberius, his step-son, took over and became the second Roman Emperor.

Claudius

He was born in Lugdunum on August 1, 10 BC and died in Rome, Italy on October 13, 54 AD. Claudius began the conquest of Britain and conquered several new areas for Rome. He also constructed many aqueducts, canals and roads.

He struggled through life with many ailments, including tremors of his hands and head, he walked with a limp and always had a runny nose. He also had issues with foaming at his mouth. Historians now believe that he may have suffered from Tourette's syndrome or cerebral palsy. His family believed this to be a sign of weakness and a source of public embarrassment.

Trajan

Trajan was born in Italica, Hispania on September 18, 53 AD and died in Selinus, Cilicia on August 8, 117 AD. His reign lasted from January 28, 98 AD until August 8, 117 AD.

Although he was born in Hispania, his father was a great Roman general and politician and his mother was from a prominent Roman family. He would spend time in Spain as well as in Rome. Trajan is considered to be one of the greatest Roman Emperors. His reign lasted for 19 years.

It was during this time that he conquered lands which increased empire's wealth and size. He was an ambitious builder, and constructed many of the buildings throughout Rome. He became ill while he was campaigning in the middle east. He died on his return to Rome while in Cilicia. His adopted son Hadrian then succeeded him as the ruler.

Marcus Aurelius

Marcus Aurelius was born in Rome, Italy on April 26, 121 AD and died on March 17, 180 AD in Vindobona Pannonia. His reign lasted from 161 to 180 AD. He ruled as co-emperor Lucius Verus from 161 until 169, when Verus died. Aurelius is referred to as the Philosopher-King.

Marcus Aurelius

He was not only an Emperor of Rome, but also was thought of as one of the foremost tolerant philosophers. He is known as last of the "Five Good Emperors". He died on March 17, 180 and his ashes were deified immediately and were then sent back to Rome, where they rested at Hadrian's mausoleum until the Visigoth sack of the city in 410. He is also commemorated with a column and temple in Rome.

CRAZY EMPERORS

There were also crazy Emperors that ruled Rome. Some of them were Nero (who many felt was the one to blame for burning Rome), Domitian, Commodus and Caligula.

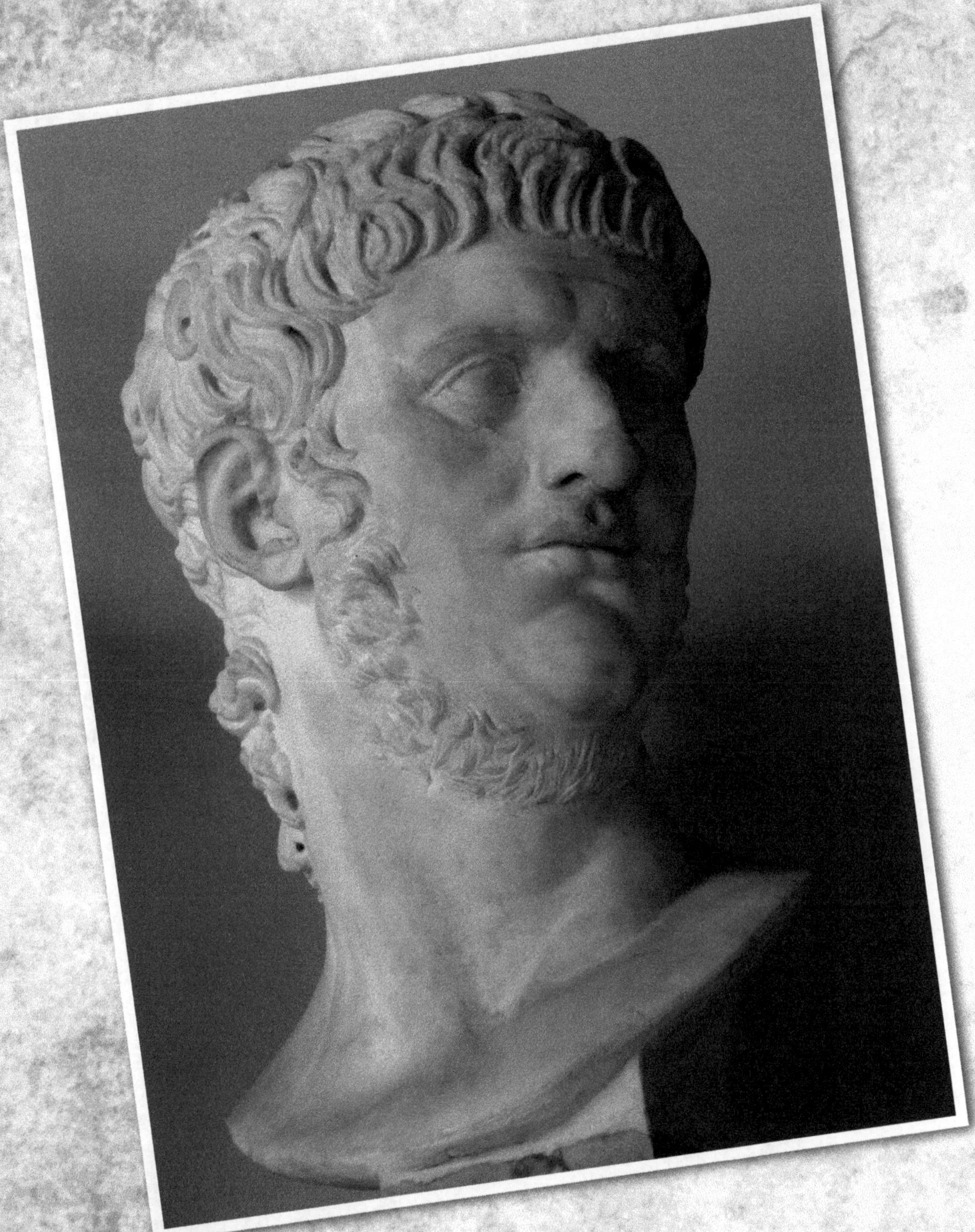

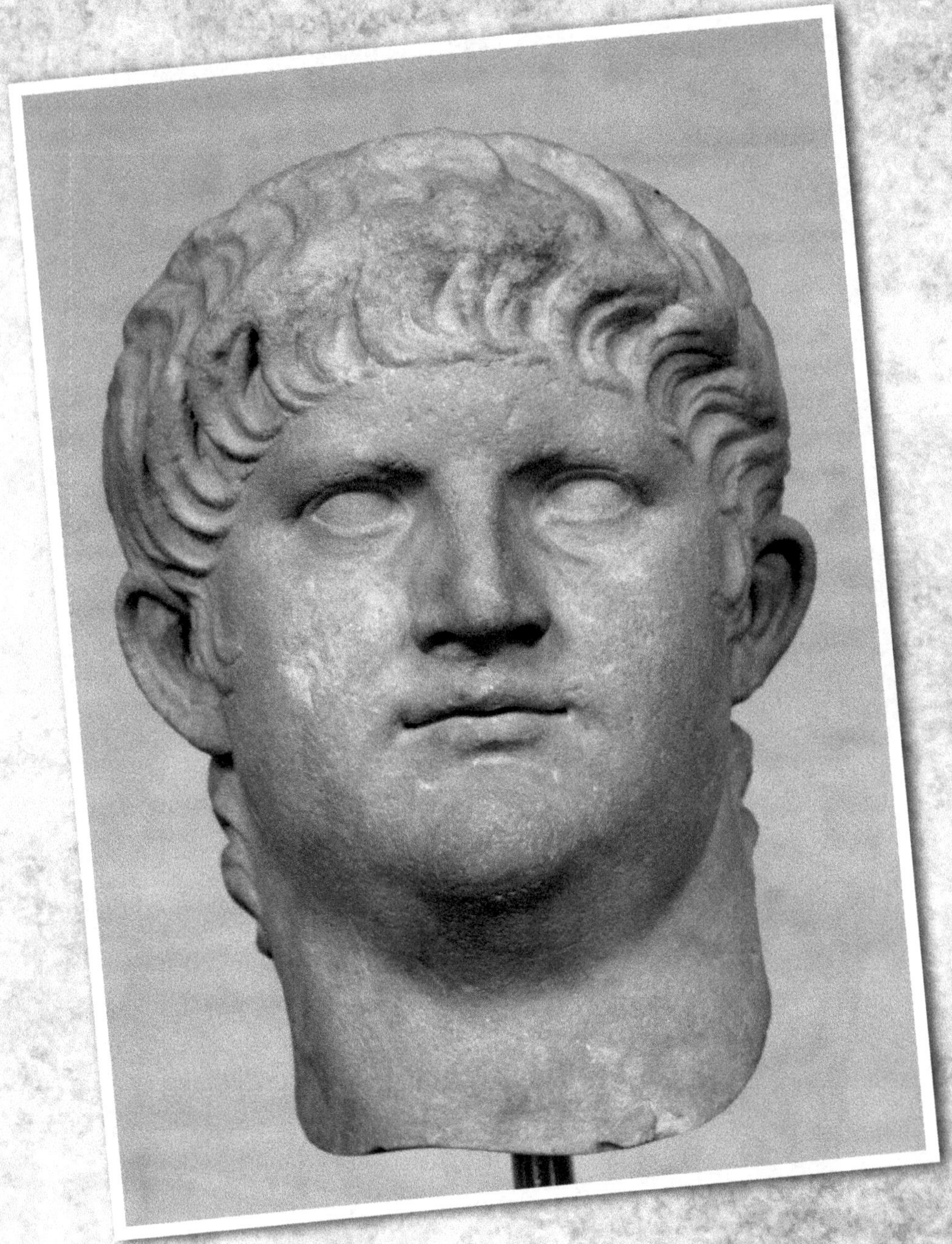

Nero

Nero was born in Antium, Italy on December 15, 37 AD and died outside of Rome, Italy on June 9, 68 AD. His reign lasted from October 13, 54 AD until June 9, 68 AD. He was known to be one of Rome's worst Emperors and legend indicates that he was playing his fiddle during the time when Rome was burning.

He was also known to execute anyone that did not agree with him, possibly even his mother. Some of the people began revolting against him in 68 AD. He then committed suicide so that the Senate could not execute him.

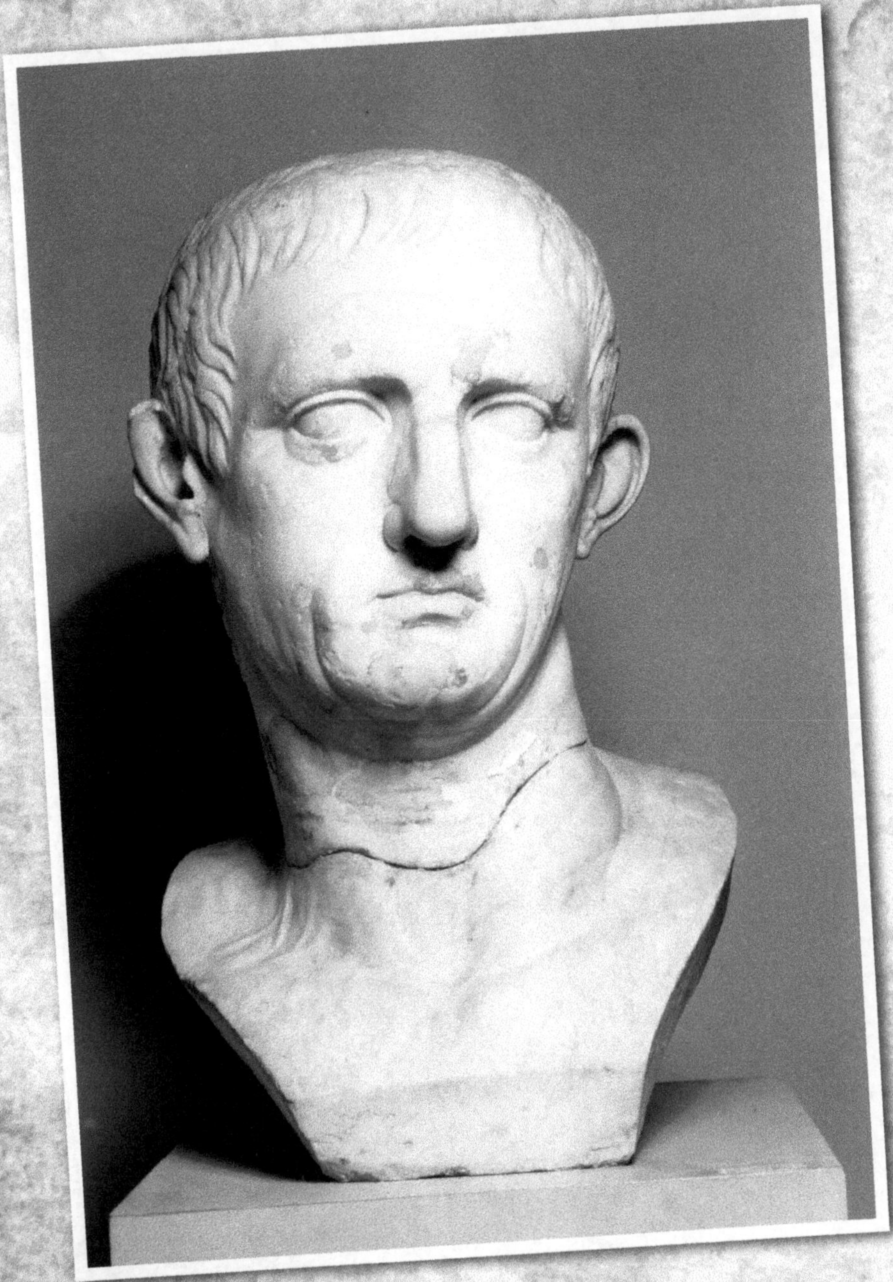

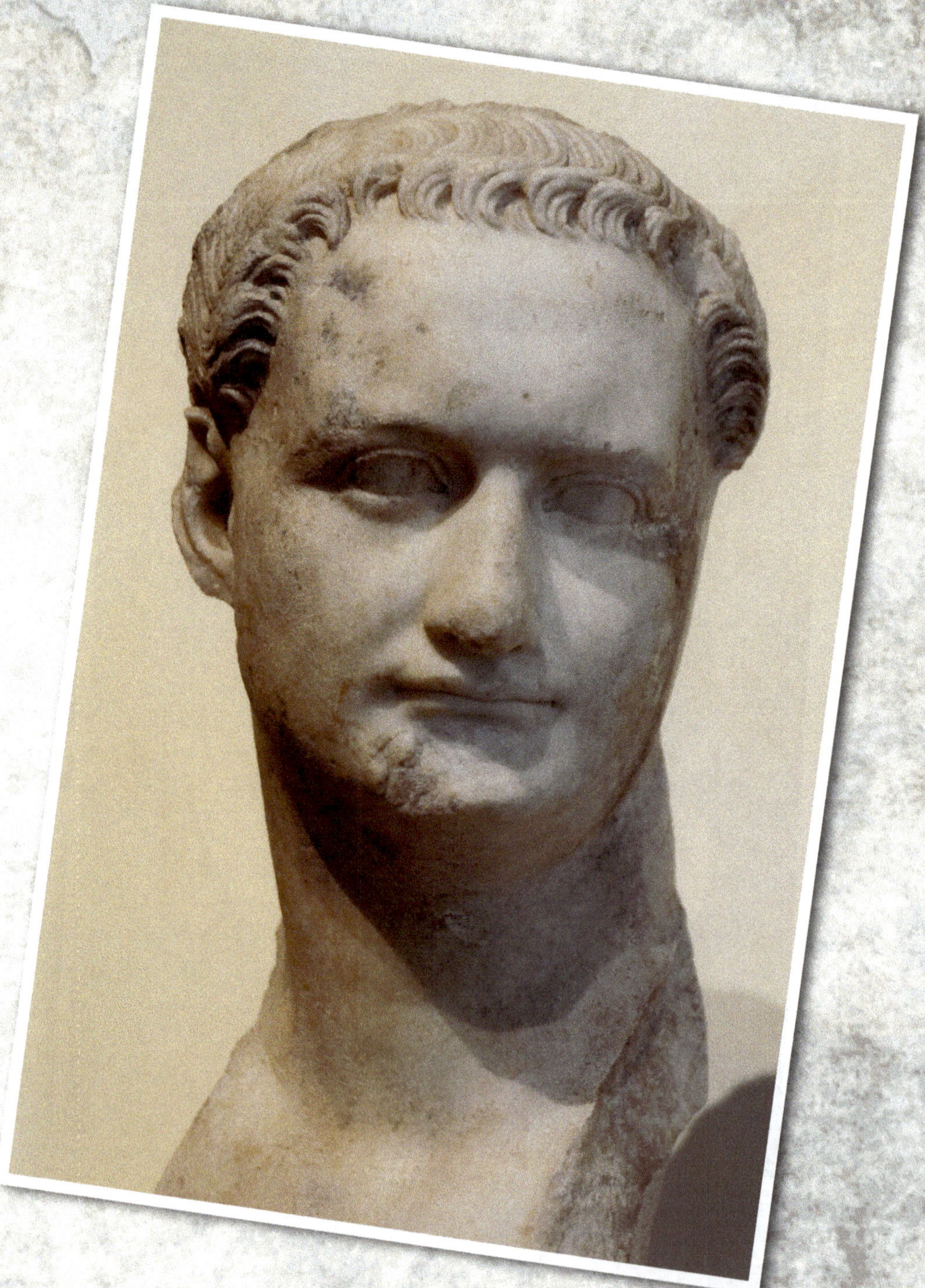

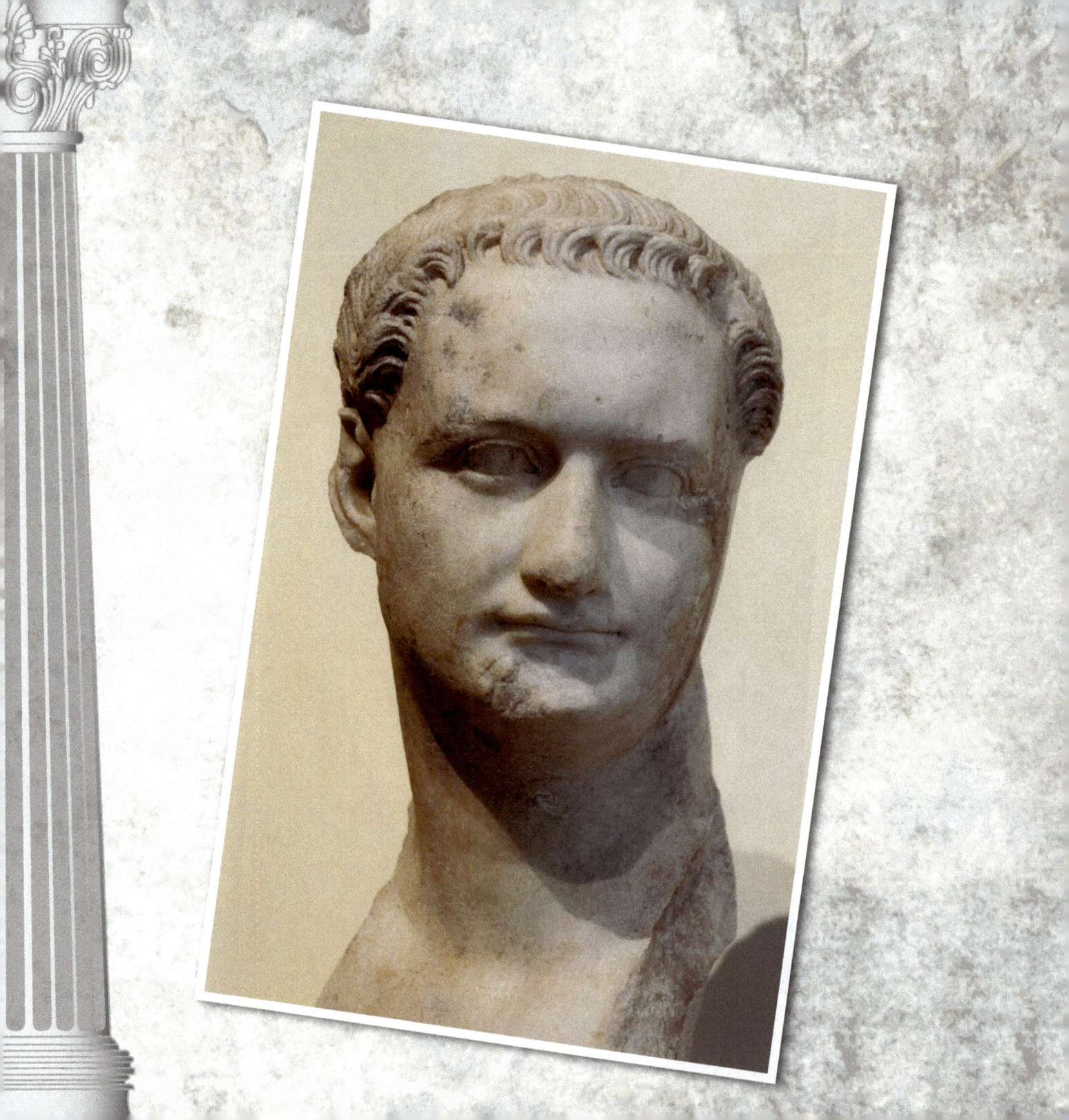

Domitian

Domitian was born in Rome on October 24, 51 AD and was assassinated by court officials on September 18, 96 AD.

While ruling the Empire, he strengthened the economy, expanded border defenses and started a major building program in order to restore the city of Rome. His government displayed totalitarian characteristics and he began to see himself as a new Augustus, destined to guide the Empire to a brilliant new era.

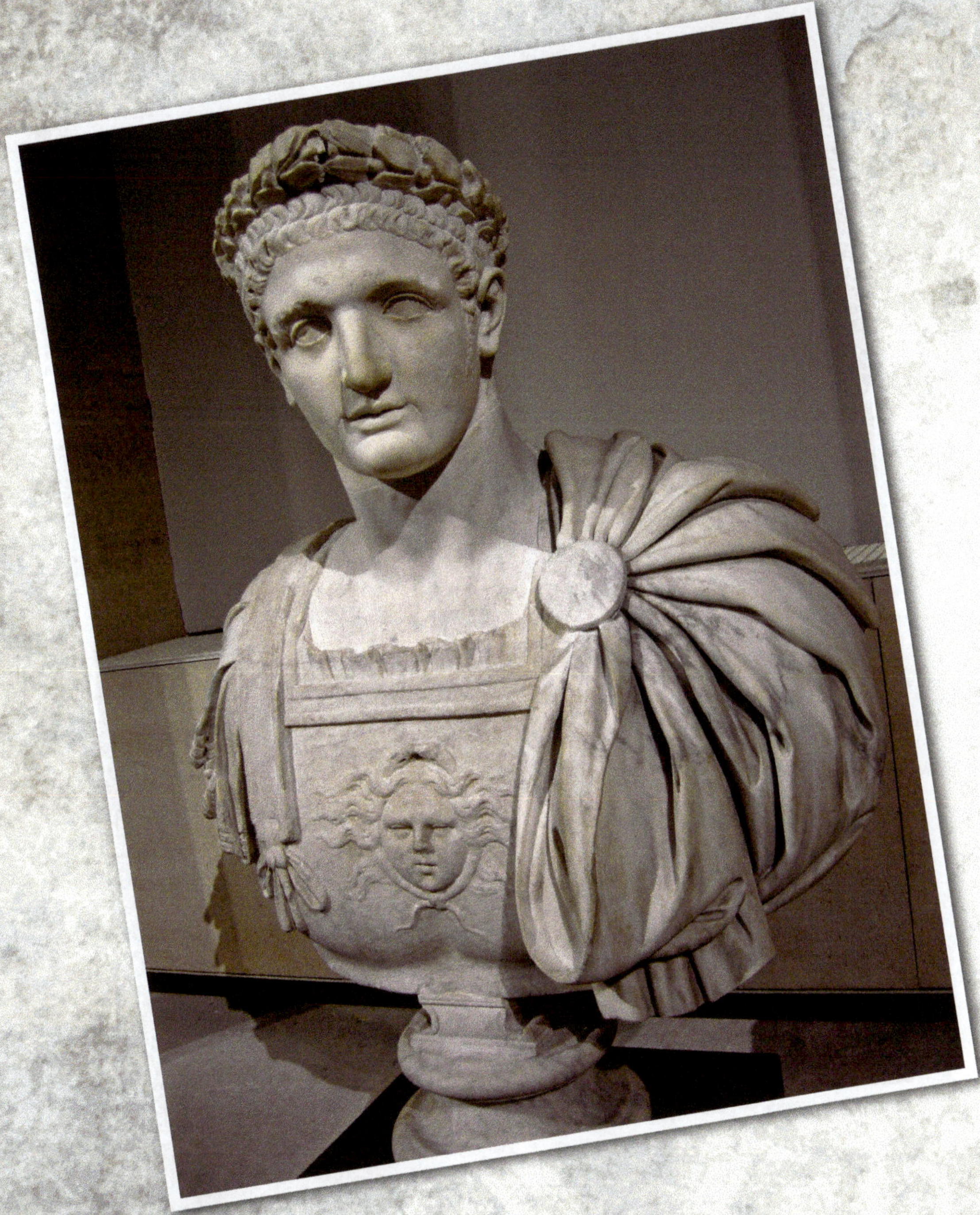

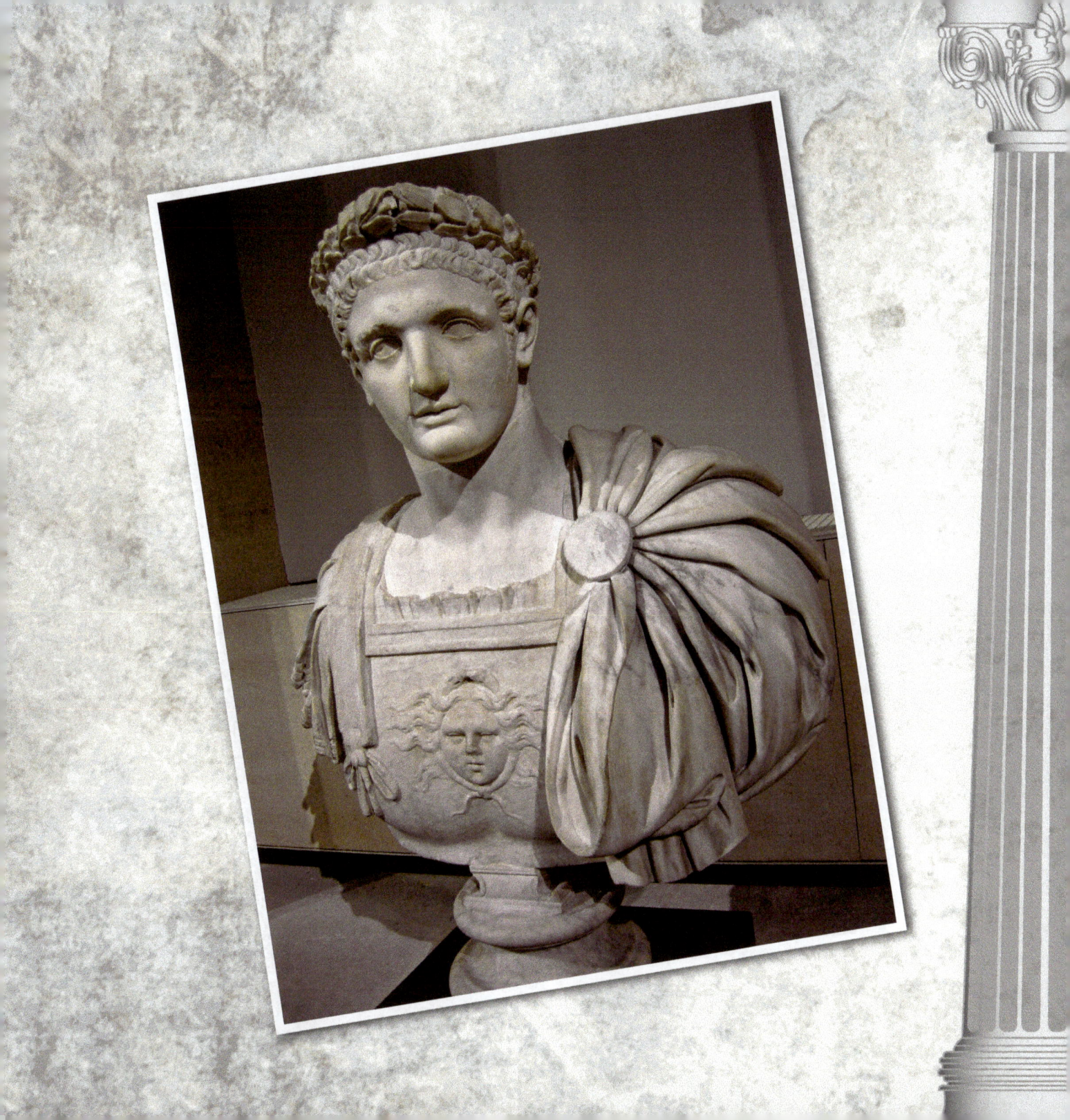

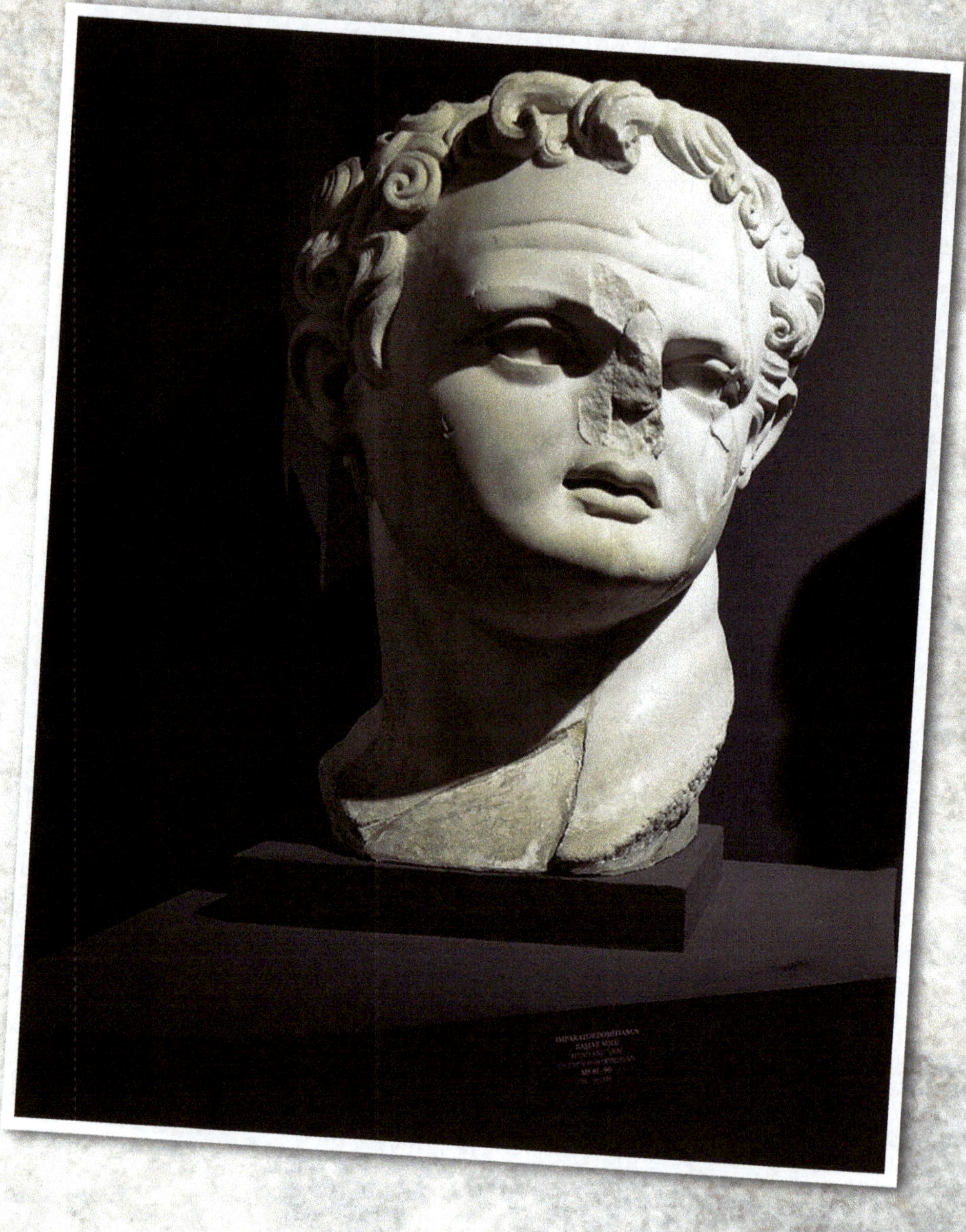

Cultural, military and religious propaganda grew into a cult of personality and by then nominating himself as the perpetual censor, he was determined to control private and public morals. As a result of this, he became popular with the army and the people, but was known as a tyrant by the Roman Senate.

Commodus

Commodus was born August 31, 161 AD and died December 31, 192 AD. His reign lasted from 180 AD to 192 AD. He ruled with Marcus Aurelius, his father, from 177 until his father died in 180.

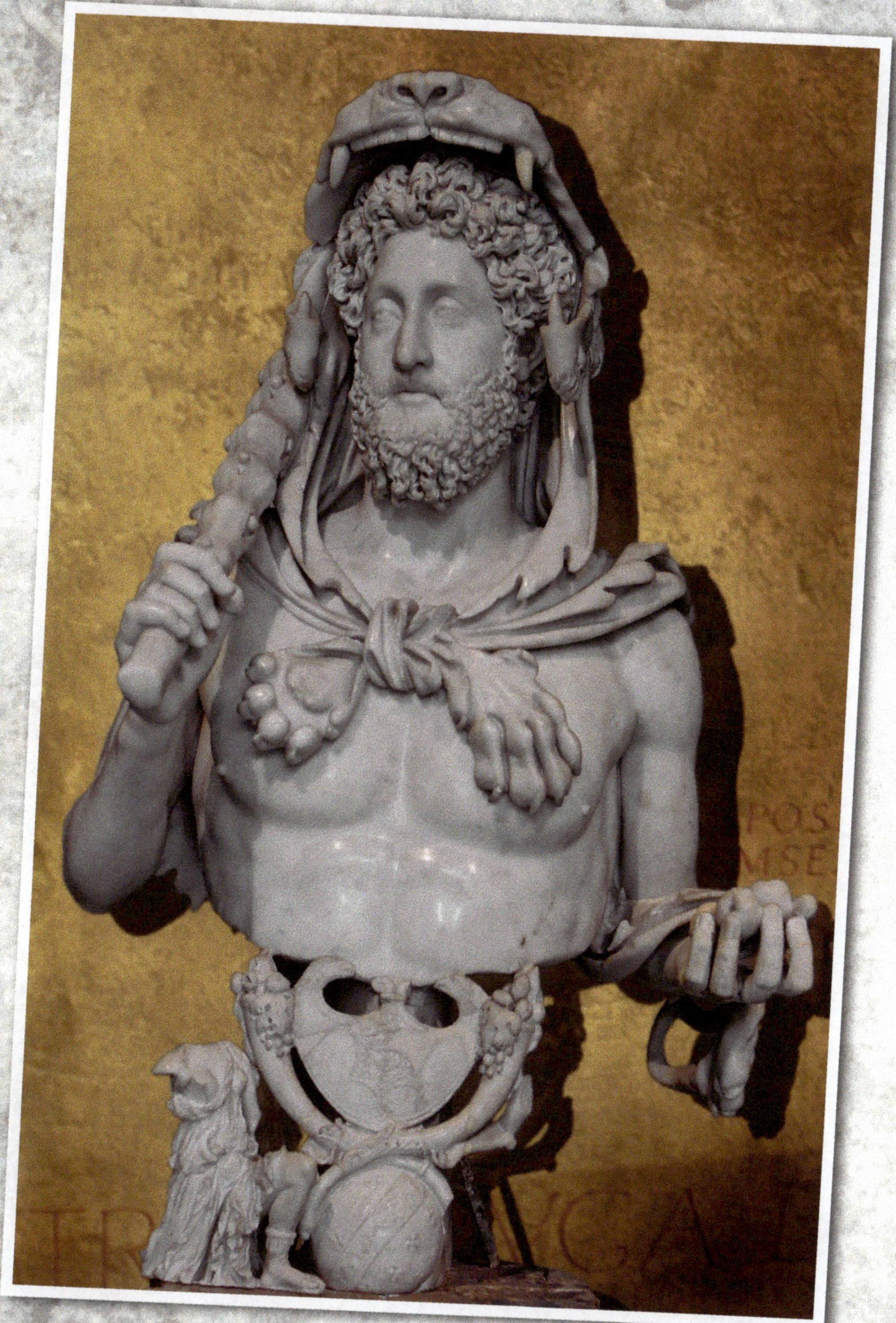

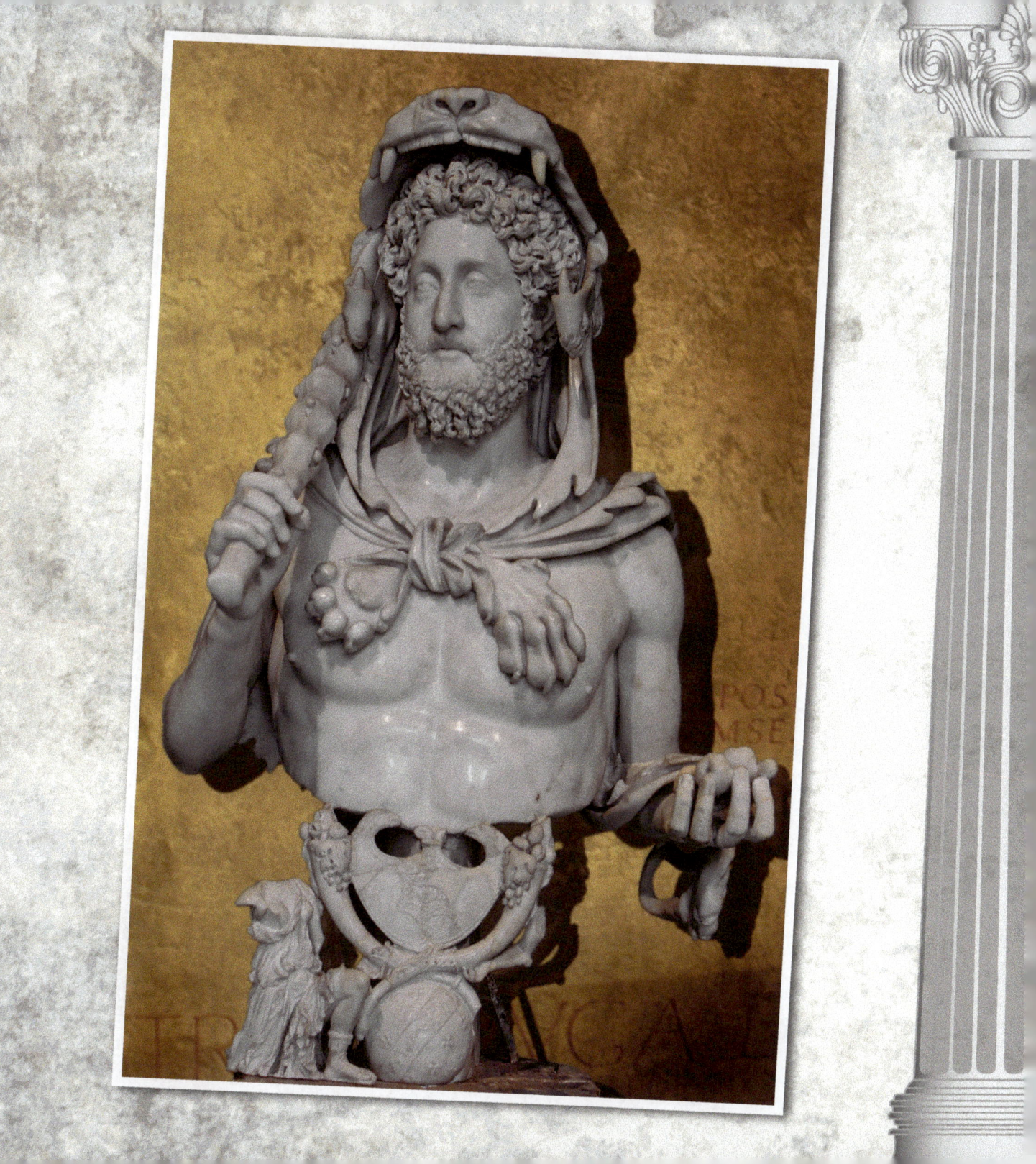

COMMODUS

A witness, Cassius Dio described him as being "not naturally wicked but, on the contrary, as guileless as any man that ever lived". His great simplicity, however, together with his cowardice, made him the slave of his companions, and it was through them that he at first, out of ignorance, missed the better life and then was led on into lustful and cruel habits, which soon became second nature.

Records indicate that his actions would tend to reject the policies of his father, the advisers and his father's lifestyle, alienating his family's surviving members. It seems as though he was raised in the environment of stoic asceticism, that which he had totally rejected when he became the sole ruler.

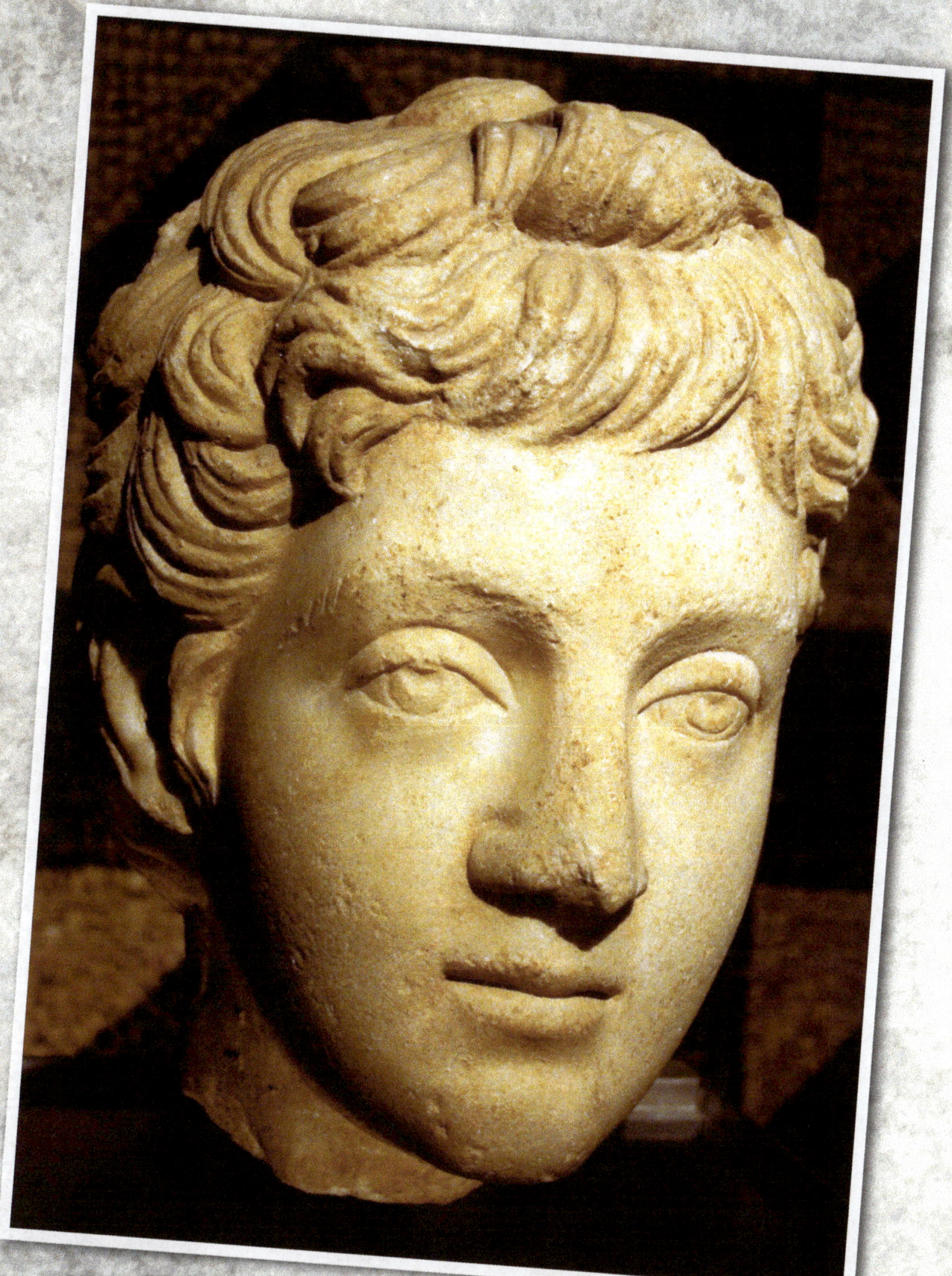

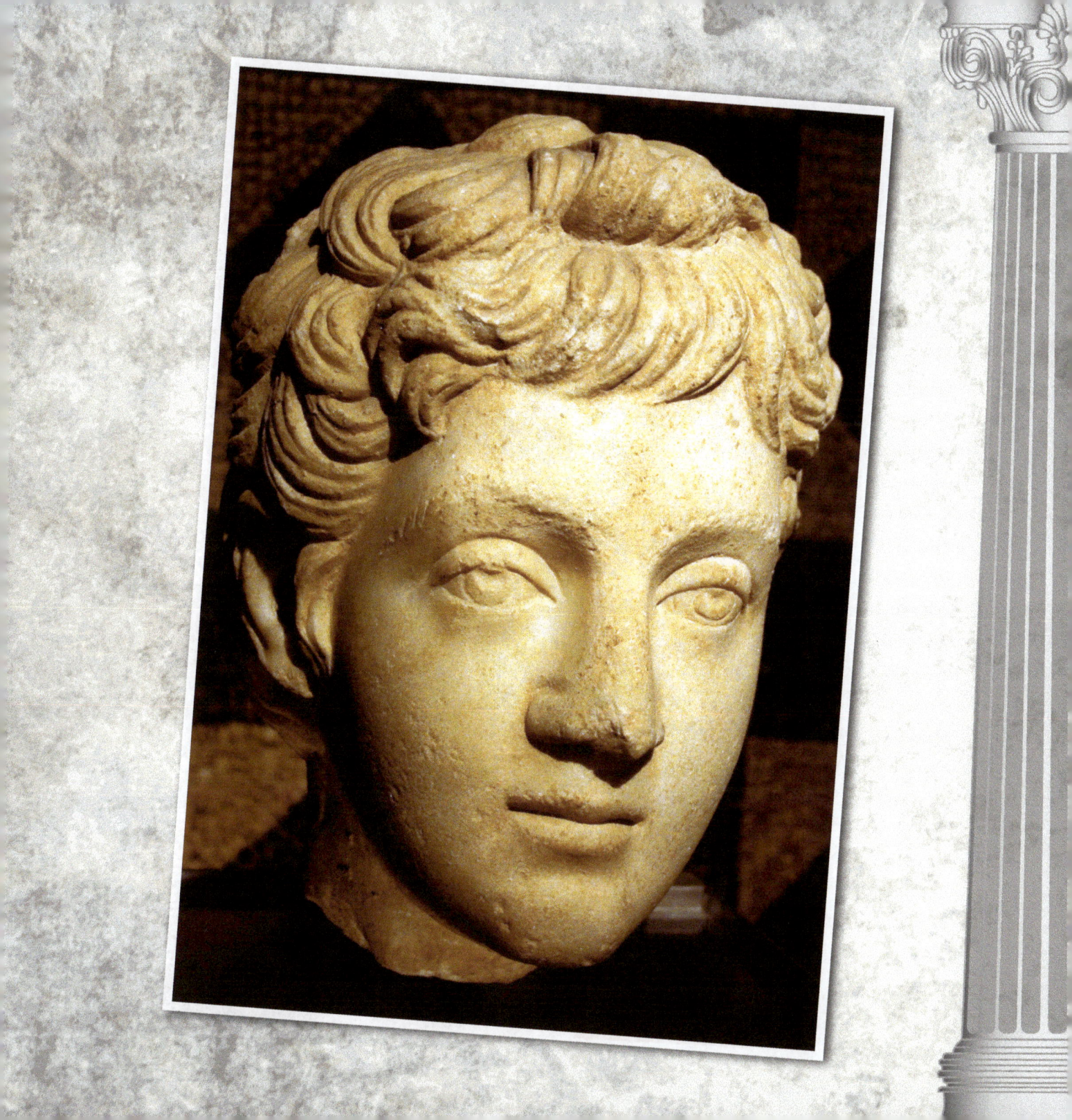

637.

Caligula

Caligula was born August 31, 12 AD, and was assassinated January 24, 41 AD in Rome, Italy. His reign lasted from 37 AD through 41 AD. He was often remembered to be a capricious and selfish ruler and his ineptitude had weakened the Empire during his reign.

If this was the case, as many scholars have argued, how did he end up expanding to the west, annexing provinces and coming up with a plan to overtake Britain?

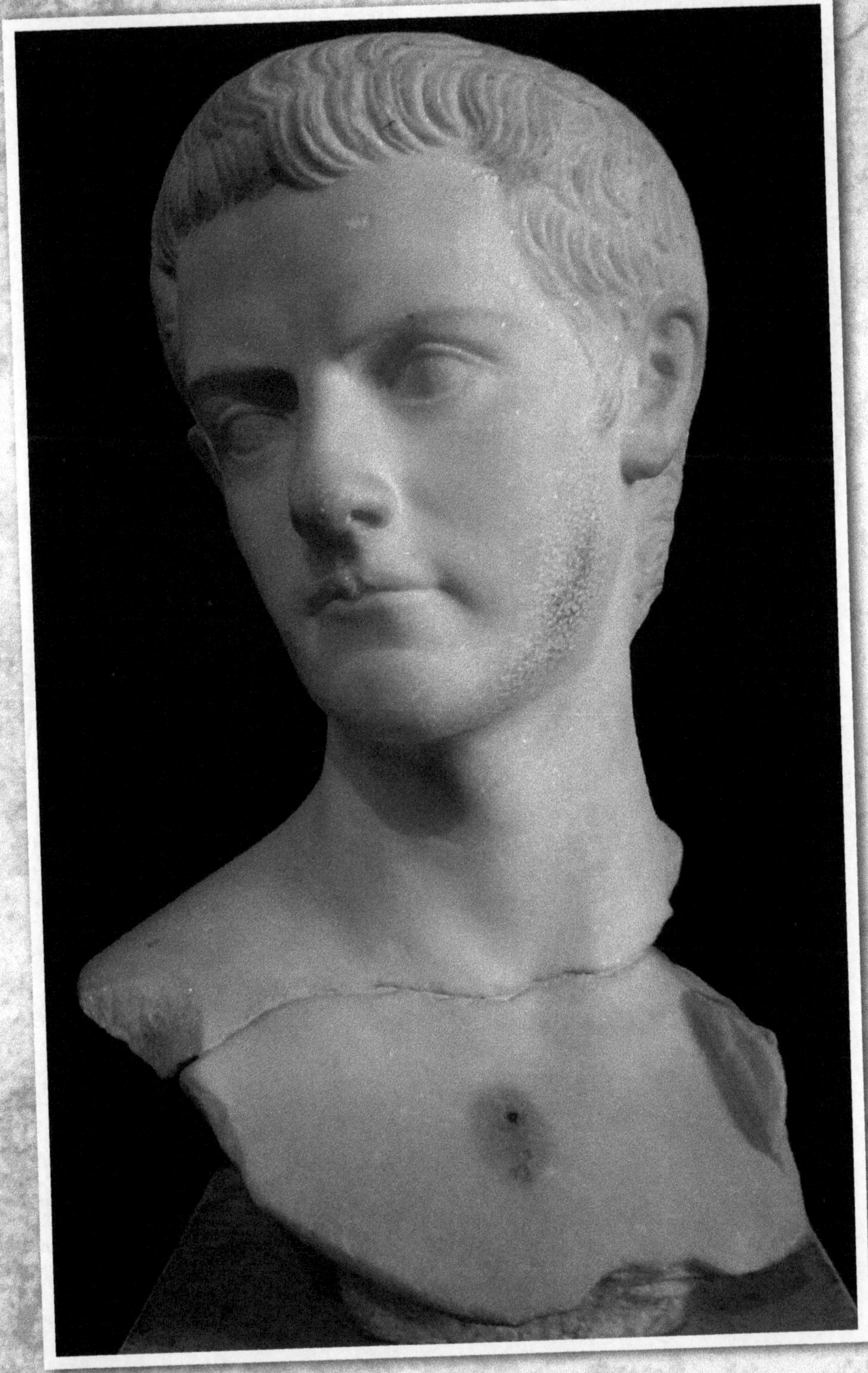

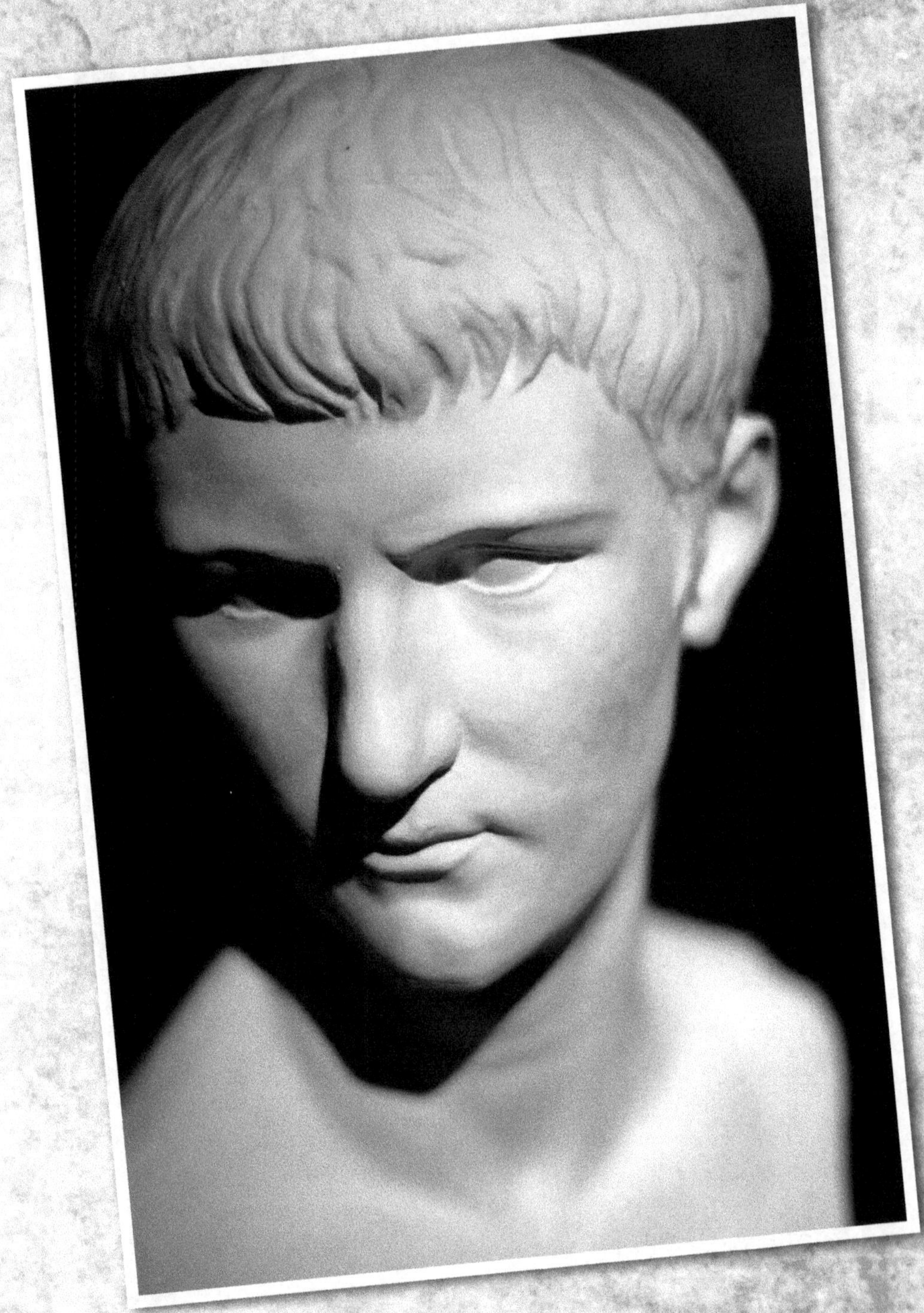

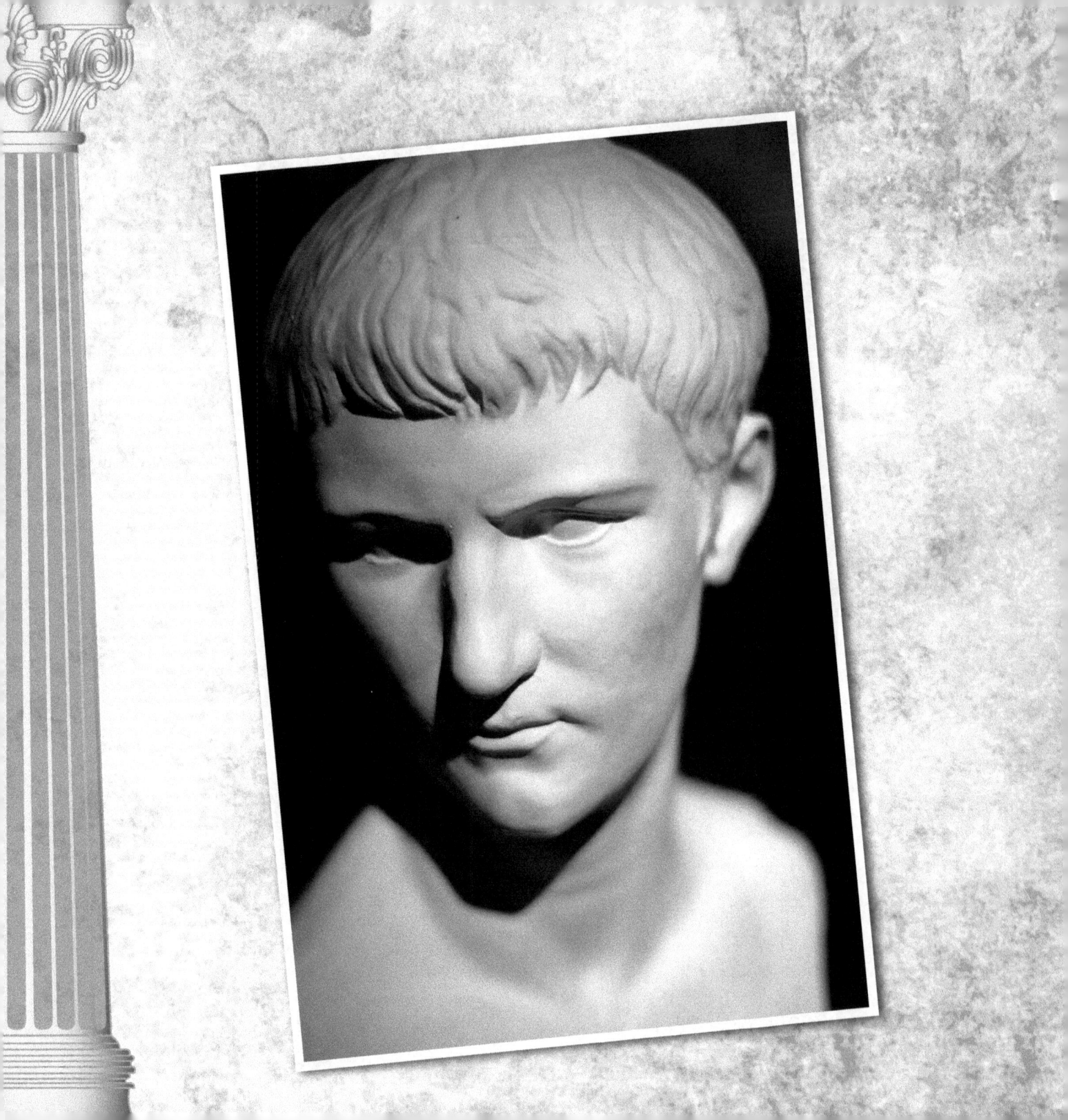

Getting no further than the English Channel, and being murdered not to long after, his preparations for an invasion allowed Claudius to begin their successful conquest in 43 AD, when they were able to overtake Britain.

Constantine the Great

He was born in Naissus, Serbia on February 27, 272 AD and died in Nicomedia, Turkey on May 22, 337 AD. He was also known as Saint Constantine, Constantine I and Constantine the Great. His father was Flavius Constantius, who had moved up the Roman government becoming the second in command under the Emperor Diocletian.

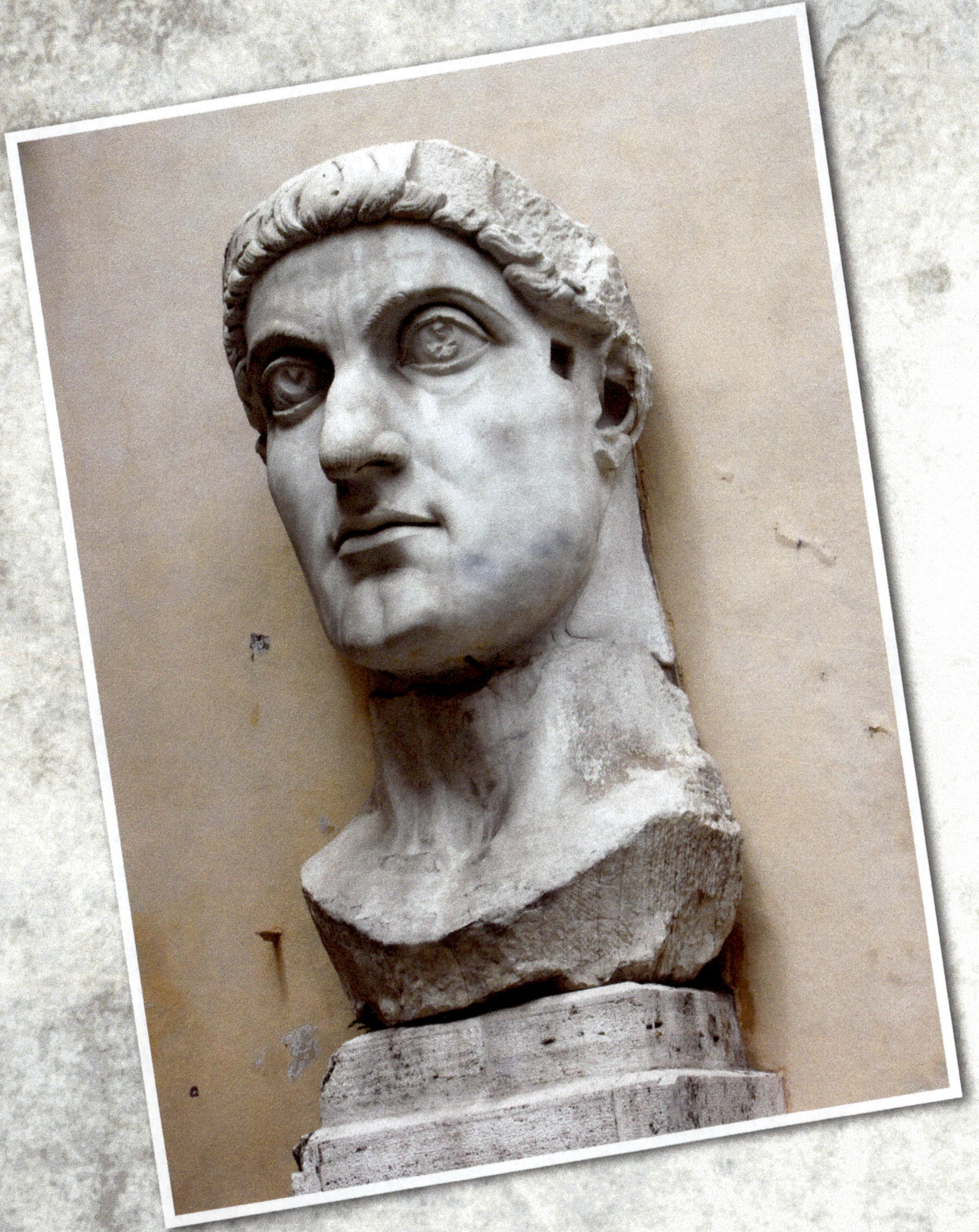

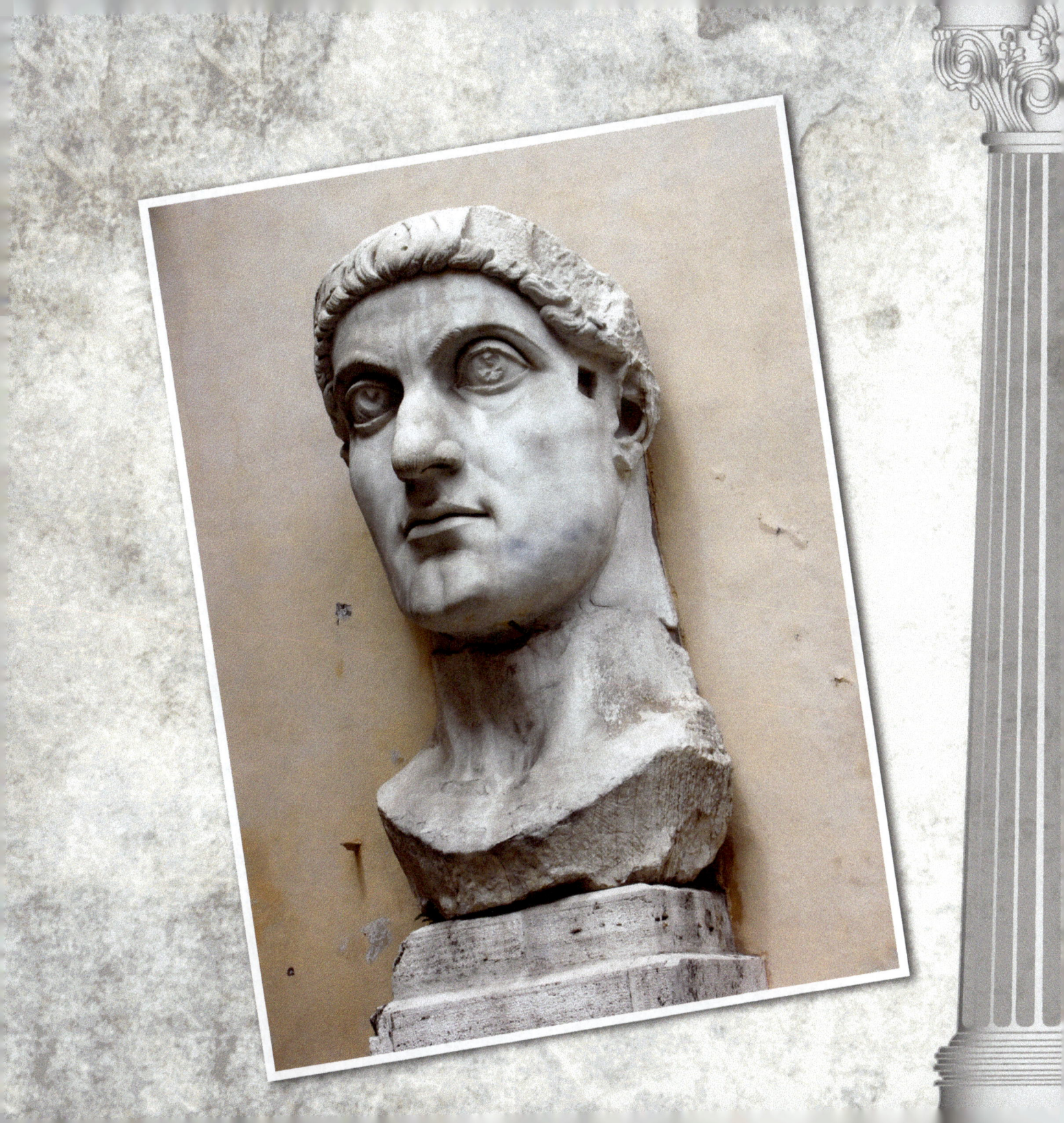

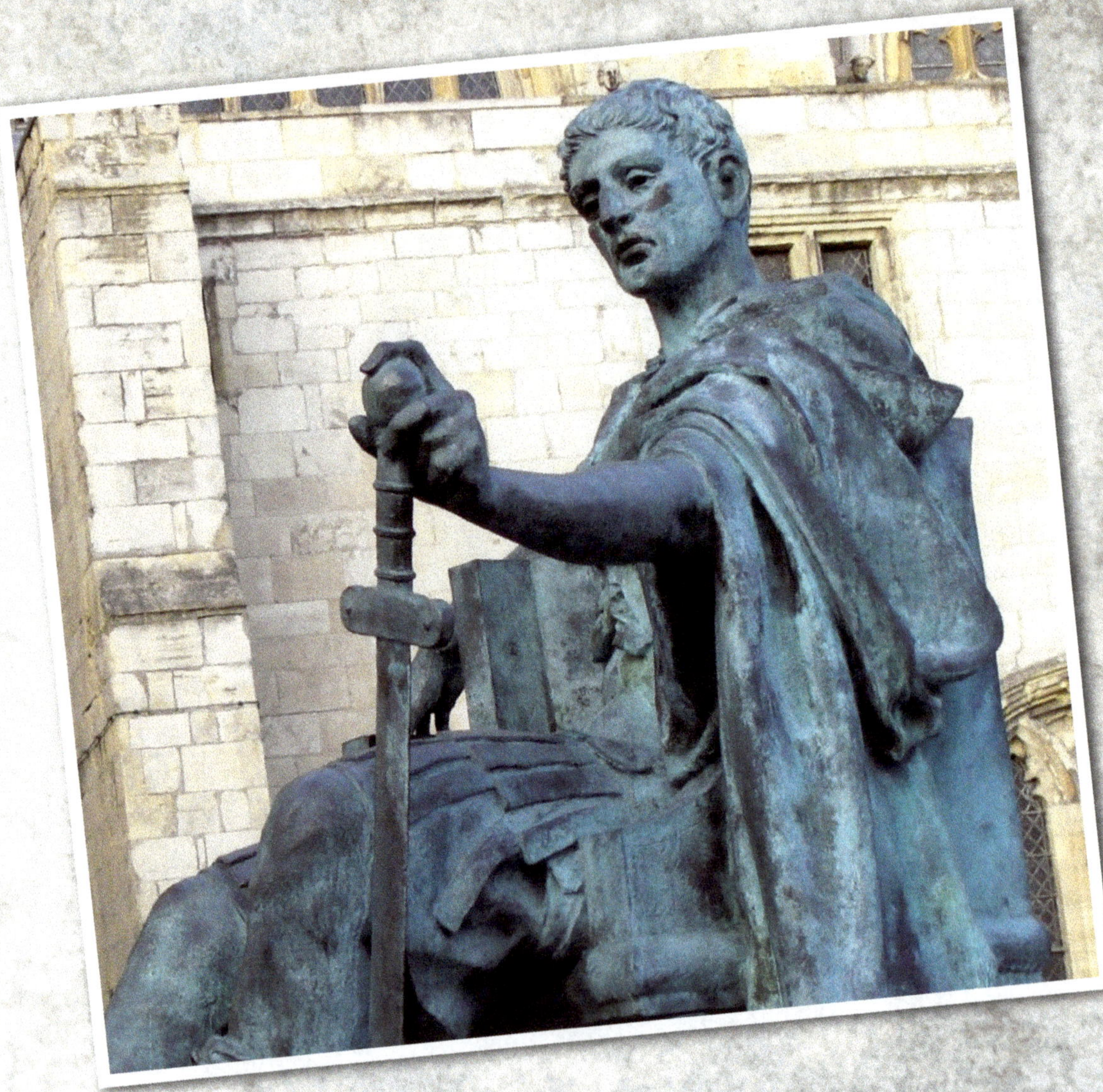

He was the ruler of the Eastern Roman Empire. He became the first one who converted to Christianity and began the Roman transition to Christianity. He was also the ruler who changed Byzantium to Constantinople, which then would become the capital for more than 1000 years. He was the ruler of the Roman Empire until he died in 337. He was laid to rest at the Church of the Holy Apostles in Constantinople.

THE END OF THE ROMAN EMPIRE

The two separate halves of this Roman Empire would end at different times. When Romulus Augustus, the last of the Roman Emperors, lost to Odoacer in 476 AD, this ended the Western Roman Empire. In 1453 AD, the fall of Constantinople to the Ottoman Empire, ended the Eastern Roman Empire.

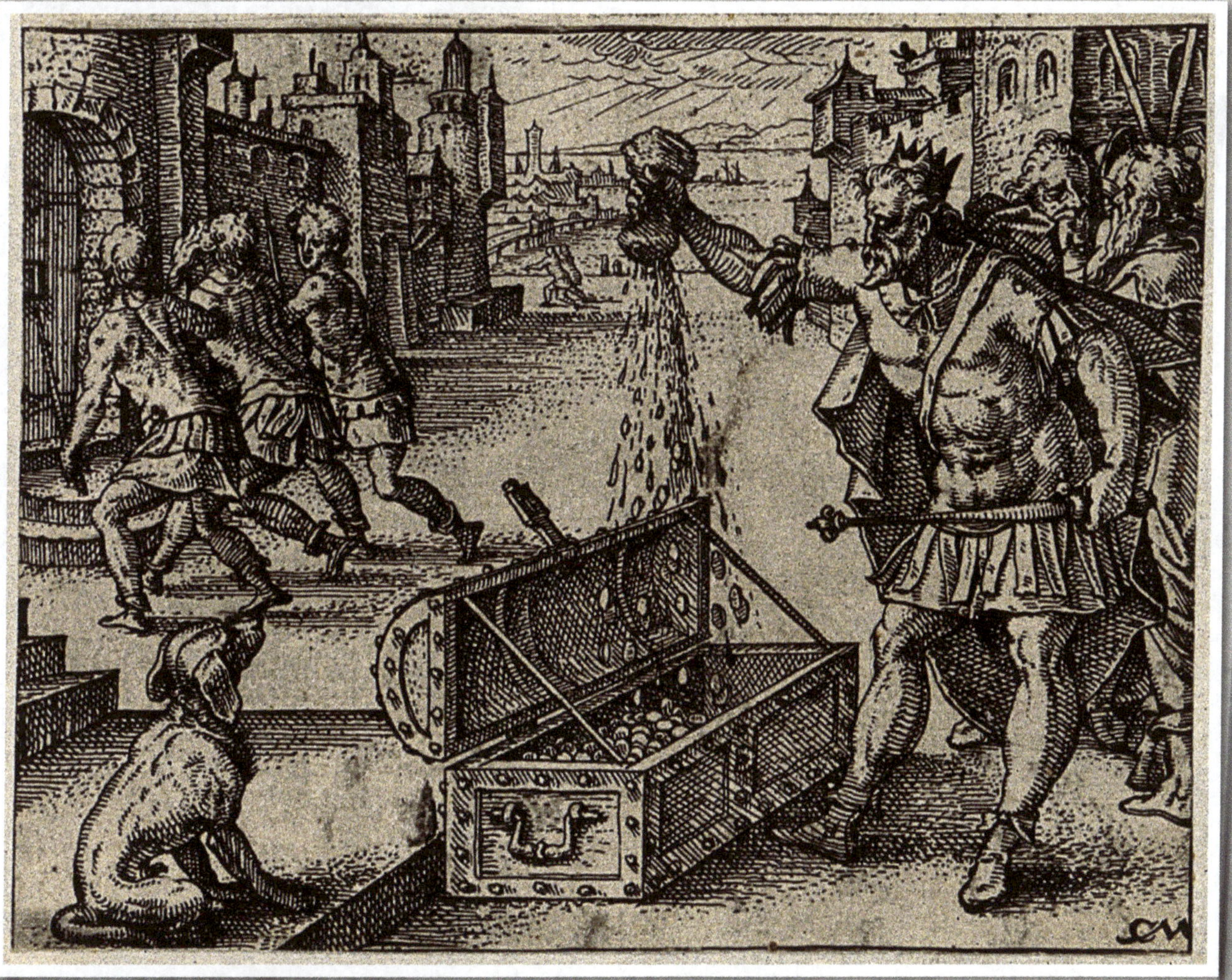

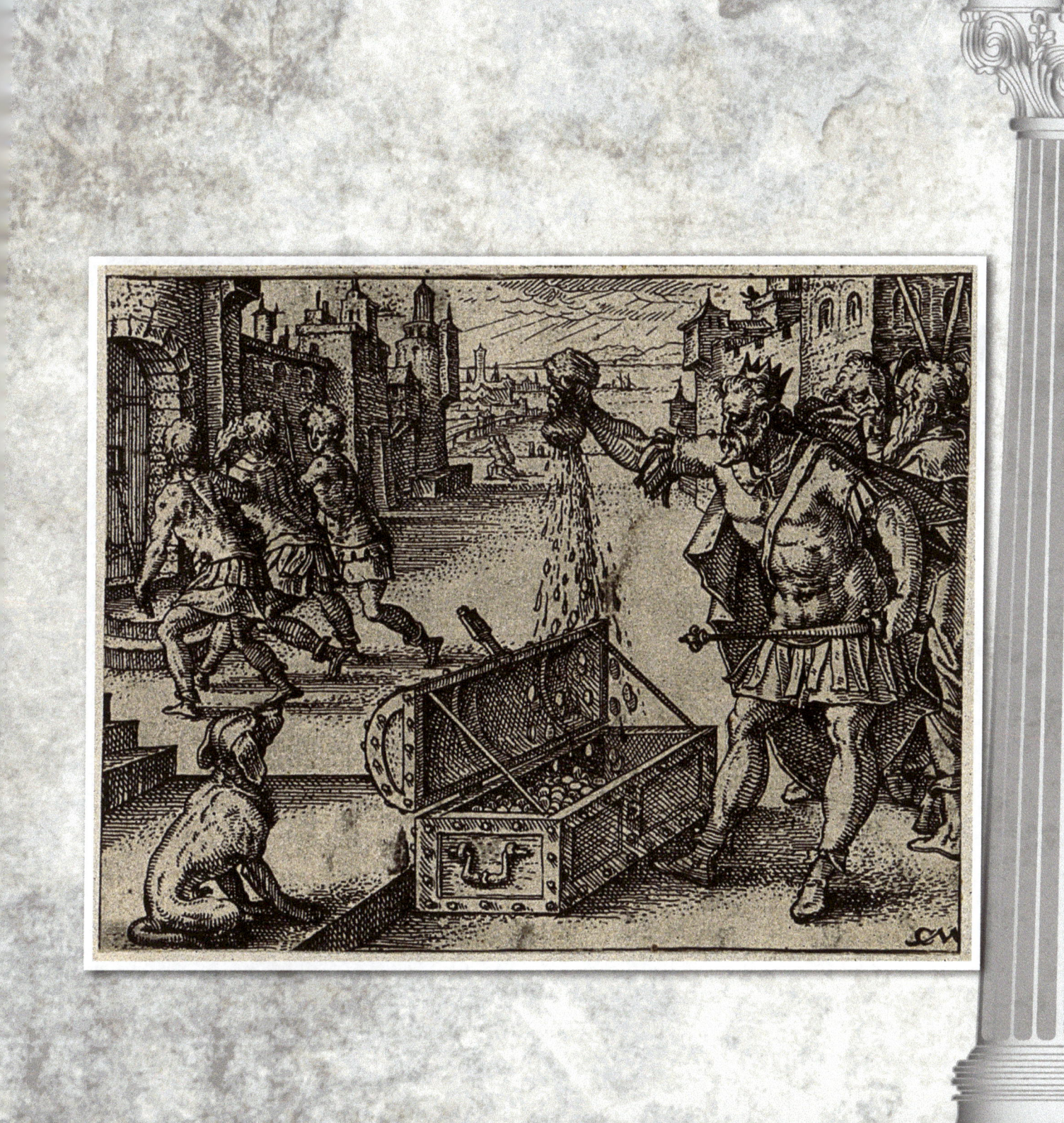

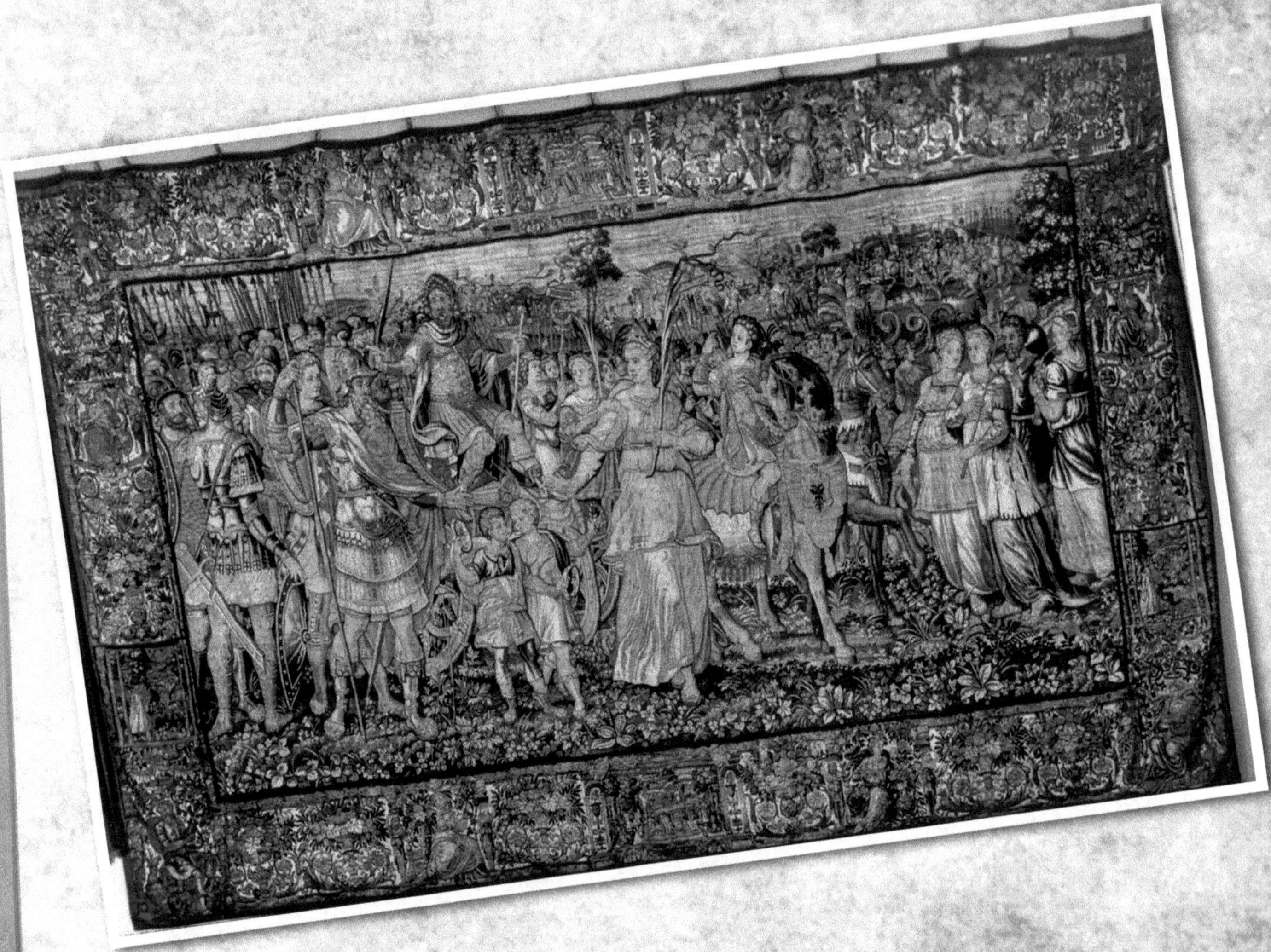

Be sure to research additional information on the internet, by going to your local library, or by asking questions of your teachers, family, and friends.

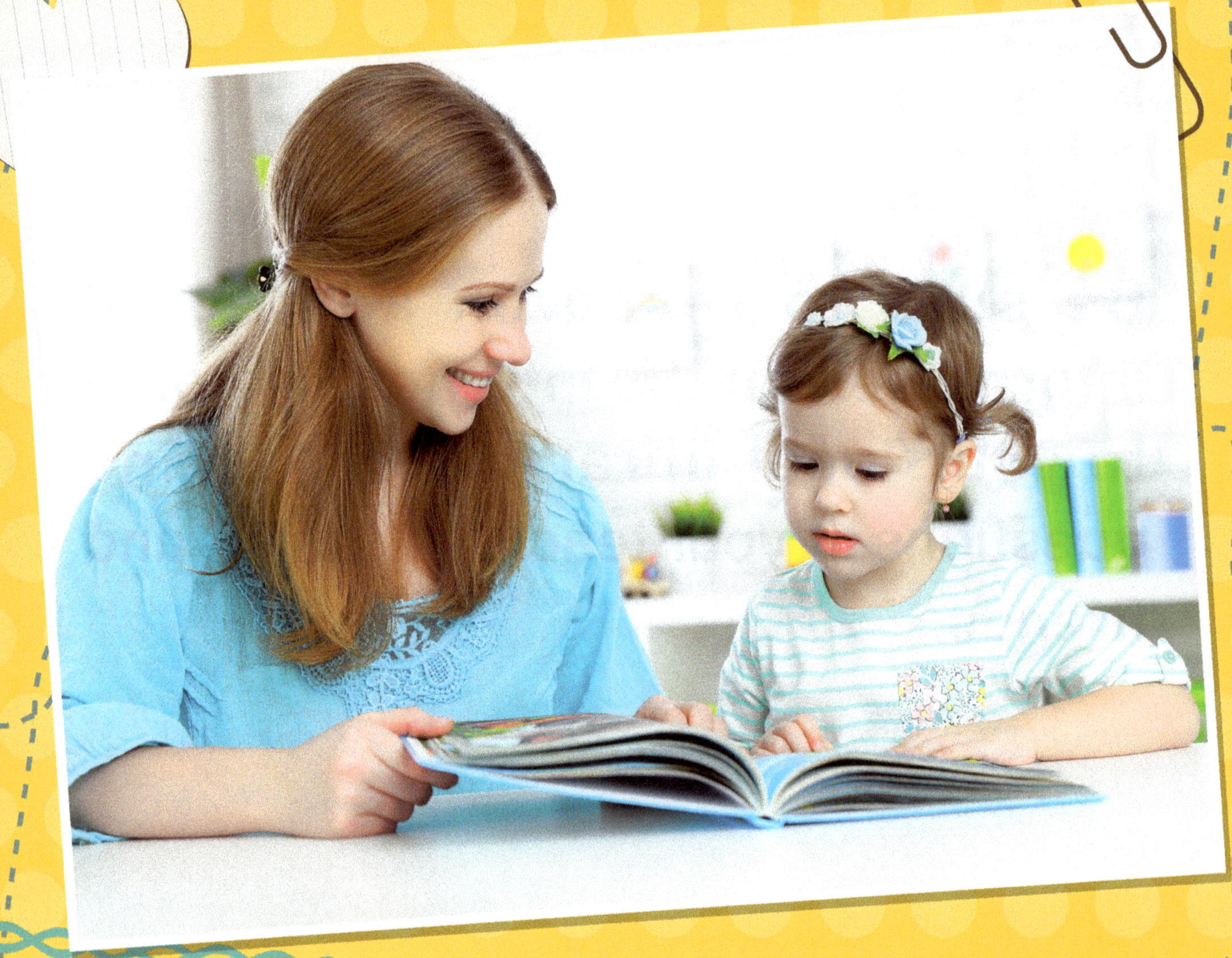

Visit

BABY PROFESSOR
EDUCATION KIDS

www.BabyProfessorBooks.com

to download Free Baby Professor eBooks and view our catalog of new and exciting Children's Books

Milton Keynes UK
Ingram Content Group UK Ltd.
UKHW051140030924
447802UK00003B/284

9 798869 416926